The Amateur Boxing Association
of England Limited

Boxing

Produced in collaboration with
the Amateur Boxing Association
of England Ltd

Produced for A & C Black by

Monkey Puzzle Media Ltd
Gissings Farm, Fressingfield
Suffolk IP21 5SH

Published in 2006 by

A & C Black Publishers Ltd
38 Soho Square, London W1D 3HB
www.acblack.com

Second edition 2006

Acknowledgements
Original text by Kevin Hickey MBE with additional
material by Alan Sanigar and Raine New (article on
women's boxing).
Cover and inside design by James Winrow for
Monkey Puzzle Media Ltd.
Front cover photograph courtesy of Getty Images.
Photographs on pages 5, 6, 7, 8, 9, 21, 23, 29
(bottom), 35, 52, 53, 55 and 61 courtesy of Empics.
Photographs on pages 13, 46, 47 and 48 courtesy of
the ABAE Ltd. All other photographs by Tim Strange.
Illustrations by Dave Saunders.

KNOW THE GAME is a registered trademark.

Printed and bound in China by C&C Offset Printing Co., Ltd.

Note: Throughout the book players and officials are
referred to as 'he'. This should, of course, be taken to
mean 'he or she' where appropriate.

CONTENTS

FOREWORD

More and more people today are actively taking part in the combat sport of boxing. From fitness and recreational programmes to competitive bouts, boxing offers unique challenges, great skills development and an invigorating means of exercise. There are plenty of opportunities for taking up boxing – there are some 600 ABAE (Amateur Boxing Association of England) clubs spread throughout England alone. Here, through careful guidance, the beginner can benefit from general physical and technical training as well as progressing, if they wish, to the competition arena. Sparring practice and more intensive programmes of preparation are available to those who choose to advance their skills.

Whether you are starting out at a local ABAE club or fighting as a professional, the basics done well are a must. Co-authors Kevin Hickey and Alan Sanigar explain in this book what it takes to be a successful boxer. Kevin Hickey (ABAE National Coach, 1969–89, and Technical Director of the British Olympic Association) wrote the first edition of *Know The Game Boxing* almost 20 years ago, and while much of the text still stands up to scrutiny, Alan Sanigar has painstakingly brought it up to date. Alan Sanigar is the ABAE Coach Educator, and certainly knows his stuff when it comes to the technical issues associated with boxing. He has been an advanced coach for more than 25 years, and for a period during those years was regional coach for the Western Counties ABAE prior to taking up his present position.

Know The Game Boxing provides an excellent introduction to boxing for a wide range of ages and abilities, helping participants to understand, practise and enjoy all the fundamental skills.

Ian Irwin
Former ABAE Performance Director

ABOUT BOXING

Boxing is a highly individual sport – one that puts all-round fitness, skills and courage to the ultimate test. Developing the technique, tactics and determination to win fights is a character-building process, as well as a physical challenge. It takes extreme dedication to succeed as a competitive boxer, but for many people boxing is also an exhilarating way of keeping fit and improving coordination.

BOXING STYLES

There is no single 'winning formula' in boxing. No two boxers are the same – champions come in all shapes and sizes, and each one will have his or her individual style. Outlined here are some of the basic boxing styles.

'Fighter' or 'Puncher'

• *Aggressive, strong, powerful*
Boxers who are shorter in stature than their opponent often use this two-fisted, forceful style. They usually press forwards, sometimes willing to take a few blows in order to move in close with powerful bent-arm punches. A 'granite' chin is essential!

'Boxer' or 'Stylist'

• *Defensive, mobile, long-range*
Stylists use footwork and long-range punching. Their emphasis is on an 'educated jab'. The stylist looks to present a moving target and to win on points rather than knockouts (see page 11).

'Counterpuncher'

• *Fast-reacting, agile, tactical*
A counterpuncher tries to make his or her opponent miss, before countering (hitting back) and then getting out of the way.

Joe Calzaghe combines a number of styles – he is a technical, high-tempo boxer with controlled aggression.

Counterpunchers are often 'southpaws' (see page 16). The more experienced members of this category can counter moving forwards or back, triggering off their opponent, as well as off their back foot.

> **The most entertaining contests are often between a stylist boxer and a strong fighter – the least exciting are often between two counterpunchers.**

'Box-fighter'

• *Selective, versatile*
A box-fighter draws on both the boxer and fighter styles, selecting when to 'box' and when to 'fight'. Many coaches favour this combination approach.

MULTI-TACTICS
The higher the level of competition, the more boxers will need to vary their tactics. During the ebb and flow of a closely matched contest, top performers can often call on a 'bit of everything' – the unpredictable style.

'Flash'

• *Flexible, unpredictable, risky*
This is the style of an unorthodox boxer – one who 'breaks the rules', for example keeping hands low and switching stance to lead with either left or right. A flash boxer has natural ability in abundance – speed, agility, a good eye and timing. But this style can fall down against a faster or stronger opponent.

'High-tempo'

• *Fast-fisted, energetic*
Usually found in the lighter weight groups, this bustling style relies on a high-volume punch rate to unsettle opponents. High-tempo boxers must therefore be super fit!

Herol Graham was famed for his unorthodox style and his ability to slip opponents' punches.

AMATEUR AND PROFESSIONAL BOXING

Although the basics of the sport are similar, amateur and professional boxing represent two very different worlds. Boxers, referees and judges in professional boxing are not allowed to take part in amateur events, including the Olympic Games.

The main visual difference between amateur and professional boxers is that amateurs (shown here) wear vests, head-guards and often white-tipped gloves.

Women's boxing is becoming increasingly popular at both amateur and professional levels.

AM-PRO BOXING: MAJOR DIFFERENCES

	Amateur	Professional
Length of rounds	2 mins (senior) 1 1/2 mins (child)	2–3 mins
Number of rounds	3 to 4	4 to 12
Weight of gloves	10 oz (283g)	8 oz (227g) up to welterweight 10 oz (283g) over welterweight
Head-guard	Compulsory	Prohibited
Vest	Compulsory	Prohibited (for males)
Weight groups	11 (see page 58)	16 (see page 58)
World titles	1	4 (major titles)

THE RULES

The rules of amateur and professional boxing are much the same, but their emphasis and interpretation can vary a lot. In general, referees of amateur boxing apply rules more rigidly, particularly relating to holding. In professional fights this is virtually ignored, and is often a regarded as a legitimate tactic (sometimes called 'claiming'), but excessive use can be penalised and a point deducted as a result.

THE WEIGHTS

Every weight group in boxing has an upper limit. If a boxer in a championship contest weighed in even fractionally over the limit, he or she would not be allowed to compete.

WOMEN'S BOXING

Boxing is popular among women largely as a keep-fit exercise. However, there are women who box competitively, both at amateur and professional levels. The first amateur female bout in Britain took place in 1997. But other countries were already holding boxing competitions – Sweden was first in 1988, while the first international event was the Acropolis Cup in Athens in 1997. And in 2001, America hosted the Women's World Championships – the first ever.

The popularity of women's boxing continues to increase, and the first National Championships took place in England in 2003. Weight categories in women's boxing are similar to those in men's, with a couple of extra divisions at the lighter end of the scale.

OFFICIALS

Competitive boxing is governed by a range of officials. Their role is to make sure the rules are followed and to decide the winner of the contest. However, their main responsibilty is monitoring the competitors' safety.

Referee

It is the referee's job to maintain control of the bout at all times. He will move around the ring, watching closely and issuing commands where necessary as the fight proceeds. The referee's decision is final and cannot be contested.

Judges

There are between three and five judges in amateur boxing; three in professional boxing. Their job is to score the contest from the ringside.

Official in charge (OIC)

The OIC is usually a senior referee, with several years of experience. He is in charge of the whole tournament and presides over the other officials.

Medical officer

A qualified medical officer has to be present throughout all tournaments, as well as being responsible for the boxers' medical examinations. Paramedics should also be in attendance during a tournament.

Other officials

- Clerk of scales: responsible for weighing in and ensuring the matching is fair and legal.
- Master of ceremonies (MC): introduces the boxers at the start of a contest and announces the decision at the end.

- Recorder: keeps a complete record of all the tournament bouts and results, and is responsible for the medical cards.

Scoring

Boxing matches are judged using a points system. Usually, the boxer who makes the most scoring blows (see page 14) wins. Occasionally, a fight is decided by other means:

- if the referee declares a boxer unfit to continue
- if a boxer voluntarily retires
- if a boxer is disqualified
- if there is a knockout
- if a boxer is outclassed
- no contest (e.g. if the ring collapses).

Amateur contests

In both international and national championships, computer scoring is used. One boxer is allocated the red corner of the ring, the other the blue. The judges press a red or blue button for a scoring blow. When a majority press within a second of each other, a point is scored.

A hand-held scoring machine is used for all other tournaments. Again, the judges use red and blue buttons to record scoring blows. At the end of the contest, the judge records the score on a score paper and hands this to the referee. Two points are added to the opponent's score if a boxer is warned for breaking the rules.

Professional contests

Professional boxing matches are scored manually. Ten points are awarded to the winner of a round, nine or less to the loser. A knock-down often wins the round – unless, of course, the opponent strikes back!

> **In British amateur boxing there are no draws – a winner must be declared.**

The referee making sure the fighting stays legal.

> **KNOCKOUT**
> A knockout result (KO) occurs when one contender is floored and fails to recover within a count of 10 seconds. In this case victory is awarded to the boxer left standing, as long as the blow that caused the knockout was fair.

GETTING INVOLVED

There are two ways of actively participating in amateur boxing: recreationally and competitively. Many amateur boxing clubs (ABCs) offer both forms, each run by qualified coaches (for UK governing bodies, see page 54).

Recreational boxing

This non-contact approach to boxing involves all the training aspects except sparring. For the young, there is the 'Kid Gloves' award scheme. For seniors there is the 'Lonsdale Golden Gloves' award scheme.

These staged skills development awards can be used purely for recreational boxing or as a stepping stone to competition.

Competitive boxing

A coach will advise a novice boxer when he or she is ready to compete. 'Readiness' is judged in terms of:

- technical ability (skills in attack and defence)
- physical fitness (stamina, strength)
- mental attitude (confidence, focus, drive).

In competition, boxers will be matched according to weight, experience and, for youngsters in particular, age.

Contact your national governing body for details of your nearest boxing club (see page 54).

Training for boxing is tough and gets you extremely fit. Many people join boxing clubs without wanting to take part in matches, as a way of getting fit.

MEDICAL CARD

All competitive boxers must have a medical card to certify that they are fit to box. Before receiving one, they need a thorough medical examination. They also have to be examined every time they box. The medical card has complete details of the boxer's record, including the names of previous opponents. This enables fairness in matching. Matches are made prior to the shows, but some are changed on the night.

EQUIPMENT

You don't need much specialist equipment to start boxing. The club will usually supply gloves, bag mitts and skipping ropes for training. For competition, head-guards and protectors are also provided.

For training, make sure you have:

- tracksuit
- trainers
- t-shirt
- shorts

RIGHT WEIGHT

Once boxers have passed their medicals, they are weighed. In championships, the exact weight group limit has to be made and maintained in every stage of the competition. In club tournaments, the weight categories are adhered to less strictly, but there are rules in place about weight differences between competitors.

- velpeau crepe bandage for hand protection and support.

For competition you will also need:

- club vest and boxing shorts
- boxing boots (recommended for ankle support)
- gumshield (compulsory and should be individually fitted)
- groin protector.

Boxing gloves come in different weights. Bag mitts are used for some equipment work, but heavier gloves are used for sparring.

BASIC SKILLS

Doing the simple things well is key to success in most sports and boxing is no exception. Well-balanced footwork, quality jabs and long-range punching and a sound, varied defence are all essential ingredients.

When learning the basics, a boxer will typically progress from stance and guard, footwork and finally punching and defences.

PUNCH PERFECT

A boxer needs to know what makes a valid punch. In competitive boxing, a scoring blow is one delivered:

- with the knuckle part of the glove
- on the target area
- with force
- while no foul is being committed.

A punch can be made with either hand.

A fighting fist

The hand is a delicate part of the body – it contains 27 bones and many different muscles and ligaments. Striking a blow incorrectly can cause serious damage. To develop a safe and solid punching fist, first practise without wearing the glove:

- curl up your fingers, tucking the tips into the middle of your palm
- fold your thumb comfortably over the fingers so that it does

A locked fist forms a solid base for punching, while the glove provides extra protection. Only blows made with the shaded area count.

Notice how the back of the hand continues the 'power line' from shoulder to knuckle.

> **When throwing a punch, keep your fist lightly clenched, then tighten it on impact.**

TARGET AREA

The target area is any point on the front or sides of the head or body, above the belt. Blows to the arms and shoulders do not score. Hitting an opponent below the belt or on the back of the head constitutes a foul and can lose points.

Lines of attack

An attack can be made with either straight, uppercut or hook (bent arm) punches. The latter are especially dangerous, as they tend to come around a defender's glove and outside the line of vision. Uppercuts are thrown vertically, in between the defender's raised arms.

not stick out beyond the line of the knuckles. Your fist should be lightly clenched until impact.

Punching in a straight line

All straight punches should aim to travel in a straight line from the shoulder. The fist turns inwards before impact, so that only the flat knuckle part hits the target. This locks out the arm and rounds the shoulder to protect the chin.

▶ The illustration shows three types of attack:
1 hooks (around the gloves)
2 straight punches (to both head and body)
3 uppercuts (to the body and chin)

> **FOUL!**
> Punches made with the wrong part of the glove or to the wrong part of the body are fouls – they do not score, and in competition the referee will caution the offender.

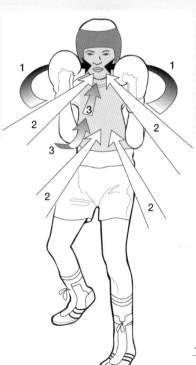

15

STANCE AND GUARD

Adopting the right stance is vital in boxing, in order to give maximum protection to the target area and provide a stable frame for punching. All boxers should stand in a sideways position, giving maximum protection of the target area with the arms and shoulders, while allowing attack or countering with either hand.

Orthodox boxers

Most boxers prefer to stand with their left foot and side facing forwards, leading with their left hand. They are known as orthodox boxers. Right-handers tend to favour this position.

Southpaws (see also pages 44–45)
Boxers who lead with their right side are called southpaws. Usually – though not always – left-handers find that this style suits them best. Many southpaw boxers are counterpunchers – they make their opponent lead, before defending then punching back. But southpaws come in as many varied styles as orthodox boxers.

 The orthodox boxer's left hand is ready to jab or guard, while his right hand protects his face and can be driven forward to punch with maximum power.

The stance of a southpaw is the reverse of an orthodox boxer.

Balance

Good balance is important at all times in boxing. Not only does it provide a stable platform, but also it enables a boxer to move quickly in any direction. The boxer's bodyweight should be transferred when taking evasive action to avoid punches. Body weight is transferred laterally when slipping, and shifted backwards on to the back foot with the layback, but should not shift too far forwards as this can cause the boxer to lose balance and can put the head in a vulnerable and potentially 'illegal' position.

HEIGHT FACTOR
Taller boxers should stand more sideways than others, to make best use of their height and reach. Their main punch will be the jab. In contrast, shorter boxers will try to adopt a two-fisted approach.

The 'on-guard' position

The same points apply for both orthodox and southpaw boxers.

Head: tilted slightly forward; the lead shoulder protects the chin; eyes look up at the opponent 'through the eyebrows'.

Hands: held at shoulder height, partly open or loosely closed, in optimum position to punch and defend.

Arms: held loose and relaxed, with elbows tucked in to protect the upper body. The arms and hands held like this is called 'the guard'.

Trunk: turned in alignment with the feet to narrow the target area.

Feet: approximately shoulder width apart, front foot turned at 45 degrees from the opponent with back foot angled further away and back heel raised; knees flexed with back leg bent the most.

FOOTWORK

All basic footwork should consist of short sliding movements, with balance maintained. Your feet should never cross or cause the base to narrow or overstretch. A good test is whether you can use either hand to attack or counter against your opponent at all times. Rhythm and speed are needed to move either into attack or away from your opponent's attack. You should aim to maintain the optimum distance between your feet at all times.

Coaching hints

- Practising facing sideways on to a mirror will help you see your stance is maintained.
- Use the lines of the gym floor to check the distance covered by each foot.

- Always keep your front foot in line with your opponent, otherwise you will punch out of distance – think of your front foot as your 'range finder'.

Lateral (sideways) movement

An orthodox boxer will generally find it harder moving to the right,

> **Remember:** '**the punch follows the feet**'. **If the feet are incorrectly placed, a faulty punch will follow. Time spent practising footwork is never wasted.**

Forward and backward movement

Moving forwards, the front foot leads, with the back foot following, and covering exactly the same distance as the front foot. Momentum comes from a push with the back leg.

Moving backwards, the rear foot leads with the front foot following. The front foot provides the drive and snaps into the 'on guard' distance as quickly as possible.

a southpaw to the left. Moving laterally (sideways) is important to both styles. It enables boxers to launch their attacks or counterattacks from different angles, as well as making them more difficult targets to hit.

Coaching hints

- Keep your rear leg bent throughout, ready to push forwards or drive a punch with the rear hand.
- Once the basic left-right movement has been mastered, you can try circling both ways around your opponent. A spot on the floor can substitute.
- Watch a video of a skilful boxer's footwork and copy in practice – don't think how it is being done, just do what you see.

QUICK CHANGE

Moving continually in one direction comes easily. It is also predictable and simple for an opponent to read. The real skill in footwork is the ability to change direction rapidly – to turn defence to attack and attack to defence seamlessly.

- Partner drills will help technical and tactical variety.
- Practise in the ring for ring control.

Movement left and right

For movement both to left and right, the same principles apply. Moving to the left, the left foot leads; moving to the right, the right foot leads. Only a few inches are covered at a time, with the trailing foot snapping into position and retaining complete balance.

The feet should maintain roughly shoulder-width distance as much as possible throughout every movement.

19

PUNCHES

Just as a skilled boxer will vary their line of attack, he will also use a variety of punches to keep his opponent guessing. There are three main types of punch in boxing – straight punches, hooks and uppercuts. Variations exist on all of these.

THE JAB

The jab to the head is the most important punch in boxing. All boxers need to have a quality jab. Not only is it the chief points scorer, but it creates the openings for the rear hand. Using the hand nearest your opponent, it gives less chance to react. Practices should be used to develop the art of feinting, with which you can keep your opponent guessing.

Throwing a jab

In a basic jab:

- power comes from drive from the floor and a quarter turn of the leading shoulder
- the arm extends at shoulder level, bringing the lead shoulder in front of the chin
- the wrist turns just before impact, to land with the palm facing the floor
- after landing, the glove returns along exactly the same path
- the non-punching hand guards the chin throughout.

A left jab to the head.

The jab to the head is the most important punch in boxing. The majority of champions, past and present, have relied on it.

Fault finder

Common faults when using the jab include:

- lead foot drift – orthodox boxers find it easy to jab moving left (southpaws moving right). This can be habitual and is easy for opponents to read. Be sure to practise throwing the jab while moving to the right (or left for southpaws) in order to acquire the skill of punching in every direction
- judgement of distance – the boxer may find themselves too far away or too close to their opponent. Be sure to use the lead foot as a 'range finder'
- snatching – not hitting through sufficiently
- over-committing – hitting through too far.

Different jabs

Once the basic jab has been learnt, different types of jabs can be mastered by varying the speed and power of the punch. Openings will occur both for fast, light-scoring jabs and for solid jabs to keep an opponent off-balance.

Coaching hints

- Practise punching at the open glove of a partner's rear hand from a standing position. Add the foot movement as soon as you've mastered the 'feel' of the punch.
- Work with your opponent moving forwards (coming on to the punch) – this will test your judgement of distance and timing, which is vital.
- Mirror work: no telegraph (preparatory movement); tidy guard; practise feinting a jab; watch both hands and elbow positions.

> **Only when your leading foot is in position should the punch be thrown – at speed! Keep your arm relaxed until impact.**

THE STRAIGHT RIGHT

The orthodox boxer's straight right to the head can be either a power or a scoring punch. Usually it follows a jab that has measured the distance for the right to follow. It is effective as a counter on the back foot, using an opponent's committed weight.

Throwing a straight right

The 'power sequence' when throwing a straight right for an orthodox boxer begins with the drive off the right foot, followed by an explosive pivot of the hips and the shoulder. This 'fires' the relaxed arm, which accelerates to deliver the final snap.

In a basic straight right:

- weight is transferred from the right to the left
- just before impact the right fist turns, to land with the palm facing the floor
- keep the left side firm
- hit through the target
- left hand remains 'on guard'.

Coaching hints

- Practise punching at the open glove of a partner's rear hand.

BACK-TO-FRONT

The 'straight right' refers to the rear, or dominant, hand of orthodox boxers. Southpaw boxers can apply the same principles to the left hand and follow the method in reverse.

The straight right is timed to catch the target moving in – adding power to the punch.

At first, keep the punch rate low (quality is more important than quantity) using single punches to a stationary target. As you feel more confident deliver the punch as part of a combination with the jab (to measure distance) to a moving target.

Delivering a straight right with full power, you should still retain perfect balance, even if the opponent makes you miss!

- Mirror work: do not telegraph the punch; ensure accuracy (you can use pieces of tape placed on the mirror as 'targets').

- Technique spar: make sure you keep this easy to begin with, again focussing on the quality. Gradually increase the speed of movement and difficulty.

- Conditioned spar: to make things more complex vary the tactics being used and the situations.

Fault finder

Common faults when using the straight right include:

- over-rotation and hitting across the target – instead of in a straight line through the target

- trying to punch too hard usually leads to over-committing and/or tight muscles, which is like trying to punch 'with the brakes on'.

A straight right on its way to the target.

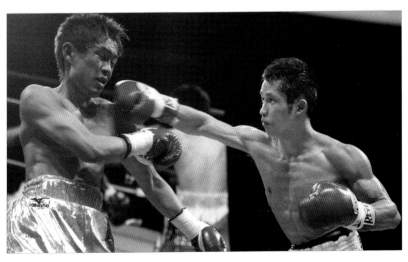

BODY SHOTS

All boxers should be able to throw a lead or counter punch to the body as well as to the head. Straight punches should be thrown in line with the shoulders and land above the belt. Power comes from the drive of the feet and the twisting of the trunk. The position of your front foot is important to ensure a solid contact with the target.

Left jab to the body

This is potentially a major point-scoring punch, as it uses the nearest hand to your opponent to connect with the largest target area.

Coaching hints

- Ensure that your shoulder is in line with the target before throwing the punch.
- Take special care to keep a high guard, especially with your non-punching hand.
- Footwork must be fast, when moving both into and out of range.

Bend your knees to ensure your shoulder is in line with the target.

- Practise moving in behind the jab, which is especially effective.

Straight right to the body

The straight right to the body is a powerful counter. It is also effective in switch-attack combinations, but should rarely be used as a lead punch.

SWITCH OF ATTACK

Once a boxer has mastered straight punching to the head and to the body, switch attacks – from head to body or body to head – can come into play. The lead to the head may be a feint, with a jab to the body being the 'real' punch to follow. A two-punch combination may involve switching the attack of the second punch to a new area.

FEINTING

Effective feinting begins with observing the responses that actual punches produce in an opponent. These can then be capitalised on. For example, a boxer jabs to his opponent's body and sees that he drops his left hand to defend the punch. The boxer then feints the same punch, causing his opponent to drop his left hand, and throws a straight right to the head where the opening has been exposed. The key to an effective feint is that it must look real – hands, trunk, shoulders, feet and eyes can all be utilised.

◀ The jab to the body is used as both an attacking and a counter punch.

▶ The straight right to the body is a powerful counter punch.

THE LEFT HOOK

The left hook is usually used as a counter punch – a punch thrown in reply to an opponent's lead following evasive action. As the name suggests, it is a bent-arm punch thrown by an explosive twisting action of the body. In the early stages, learning to throw the punch at an angle of 45 degrees to the floor should develop the right action. The knuckle part of the glove must be in contact with the target as it lands.

Throwing a left hook

The 'power sequence' when throwing a left hook for an orthodox boxer begins with the drive off the left foot, followed by a rotation of the left hip and side, through the shoulder and a final whip of the bent arm.

In a basic left hook:

- drive off the floor
- let the body pull the arm through
- feel the arm relax until just before contact with target
- the left arm retains the 90 degree bend throughout
- the punch is thrown around a firm right side 'hinge', and weight is transferred to the right leg

> **When throwing a left hook, feel the body pull the relaxed arm through.**

 The angle of the hook depends on the position of the opponent's guard. This is a 45 degree angled 'steep' hook.

- keep chin tucked behind the left shoulder, and eyes raised watching the punch as it lands
- protection comes from the high guarding right glove, with the elbow protecting the body.

Coaching hints

- With a partner, practise the hook as part of a combination or as a counter punch. For counter practice, slip inside the left jab or outside the right jab of a southpaw. For combination work, practise hooking off the jab or switching from body to head.
- Mirror work: use the mirror to focus on the start and end of the punch. Tape spots on the mirror where the punch should start and finish and follow these to ensure that you don't 'wind up'

the punch (at the start) or overcommit (at the end).

- Sparring with a variety of partners will help you to develop tactical awareness and variation.
- Southpaw boxers should follow the same coaching points for the right hook.

> **SURPRISE IS THE KEY**
> The hook is particularly effective because it comes from outside the line of the opponent's vision.

In contrast, this hook is thrown parallel to the floor. Also, note the firm right-side 'hinge'.

UPPERCUTS

Uppercuts with either hand are mechanically different to the straight and hook punches (which are thrown by pivoting around a central axis). The uppercut is thrown in a 'upward surge' from the floor, following the drive from the right or left leg. With the basic mid-range uppercut the arm follows a vertical path, while keeping a 90 degree bend.

> **Practice – with partners and coach pads – is the key to developing a good uppercut.**

Throwing an uppercut

In a basic mid-range uppercut:

- power comes from the explosive drive off the legs and hips, adding to the final whip of the arm
- the arm maintains a 90 degree bend with the palm facing the puncher throughout
- the punch drives up the entire centre line of the body
- a defensive guard is maintained with the non-punching arm.

Coaching hints

- The vertical surfaces of traditional punch bags are not ideal for training – wall bags with tailor-made indented surfaces make far more realistic targets.

- Partner work and coach pads provide the best practice, because they offer you a variety of situations.

- Mirror work is essential. Use it to check your technique, i.e. the vertical path, and that there is no obvious telegraph or big wind-up to the punch that will act as a signal to your opponent.

QUICK AND CLOSE

Uppercuts are mainly counter punches, ideal against a leaning or crouching opponent, or as part of close-range combinations (see page 40). Like hooks, they can take an opponent by surprise, as they come from an unseen direction.

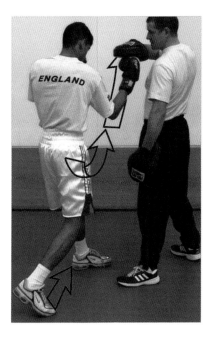

ABOVE: For an orthodox boxer, a right uppercut to the head involves drive from the right foot.

ABOVE RIGHT: The force of a left uppercut to the head travels up through the left leg and hip.

Here the uppercut is used as a counter against a committed attack.

DEFENCES AND COUNTERING

The art of boxing is to hit your opponent without being hit yourself. A boxer should acquire as many defensive techniques as possible, in order to be prepared against any type of opponent. It is also vital to be able to counter (punch back). There are several defences that can be used against any one punch – e.g. there are 11 that can be used against the jab. Similarly, most defences can be used against several punches – e.g. the push away.

An outside parry to the left jab deflects the fist off line before it meets the target.

METHODS OF DEFENCE

There are numerous defence variations, but most of them fit into three main areas:

1 blocks and parries – using the hands, arms and shoulders to block or deflect punches

2 defensive footwork – making small movements to get out of range, for example push-aways, sidesteps and pivots

3 evasive body movements from the waist, for example ducking and slipping.

These are explained in more detail on the next pages.

General rules

Some general tips for defence in boxing are:

- keep defensive moves 'small' – don't reach out with a block; slip just outside a punch; push just out of range

- where possible, take your target outside your opponent's line of attack, as in the sidestep

- keep your balance at all times, so you are ready to defend a possible second or third punch

- positive defence – the end position of many defensive moves involves a transfer of body weight; this should be used to add power to any counter punch.

Coaching hints

- Practise each defence separately, with a partner attacking at controlled speed. Gradually, as your confidence increases, the attacking punch can be thrown at a realistic speed.
- Even on equipment where no punches are thrown at you, you can still practice defence – for example staying alert while moving away after attacking the bag.
- Work with different partners, who will have different tactics and timing.

This elbow block neatly prevents a jab to the body. To block a punch, any part of the arm can be used, but it should remain close to the body.

With the eyes on the target and the high gloves in front, the head is in a balanced and 'legal' position.

Leave your defensive move as late as possible. That way, your opponent will be committed, and you can launch a counterattack.

BLOCKS AND PARRIES

Blocks should be small and compact, returning at speed to the on-guard position. Parries should be fast deflections. There are two key points to remember:

- when blocking body punches, turn the trunk to move the elbows – if the arm is moved by itself, this leaves the chin exposed
- in most situations, the hand not used to defend will be used for the counter.

The block or 'catch'. Wait, don't reach – let the jab come to you. It is a movement across rather than forward.

FOOTWORK DEFENCES

An elusive target moving in unpredictable patterns is difficult to read. Add lightning switches to attack or counter, feints and speed changes from all angles.

- Push away – push off the front foot; the back foot moves first and the front foot follows the same distance.
- Push back – push off the back foot with the front foot leading into range.
- Angles – steps across, sidesteps and pivots are particularly effective against committed attacks.

Sidestepping against a left jab causes the attacker's punch to slip past the defender's ear.

EVASIVE ACTION FROM THE WAIST

This is a positive defence that leaves both hands free to counter.

- Ducking – 'squash in' at the trunk, and bend knees to duck the head just below the attacking punch. Keep your hands high and eyes on the target.
- Slipping – rotate at the waist and transfer body weight to slip the head either inside or outside the attacking punch. Keep your hands high and eyes on the target.
- Layback – the head is taken out of range by the trunk leaning backwards from the small of the back and increasing the degree of bend in the rear leg ('sitting back').

A push-away against a left jab to the head.

When slipping inside a left jab to the head, the defender's weight shifts on to the left foot; when slipping outside it shifts on to the back foot. Note that the guard remains high and the balance is kept despite the upper body movement.

COVERING

A sudden two-fisted attack can often force a boxer into a corner of the ring to regain his or her composure. There will be an immediate need to go on the defensive, before deciding on a counterattack. Covering provides the defence needed.

> **BUYING TIME**
> In competition, covering helps a boxer to 'buy some time' when he or she is in difficulty.

Types of cover

There are three basic positions to adopt as a cover:

1 full cover

2 half cover

3 cross cover.

1 In full cover – both hands are held high, with elbows close to the sides. Round off shoulders, chin tucked in, eyes remain on the opponent. Add movement from the waist.

2 Adopting a half cover position – turn the trunk sideways and body weight shifts to the back leg. The left side is protected by raised left shoulder, chin is tucked in, and left arm guards the body. The right side is protected by the right arm and glove.

3 The cross cover – the head is protected by the bent right forearm, chin tucked in. Body is covered by the left forearm – the ideal counter would be a left hook.

Coaching hints

- Try each form of cover before deciding which best suits your individual style and build.

- Practise with a partner throwing light punches at you – this will soon build up the confidence you need.

- Add movement from the waist – weaving and rolling – making the target more elusive.

- Practise counters, starting with single punches.

- Turning the opponent requires care – make sure pushing (a foul) is not involved. Practise fast pivots to left or right, deflecting the attacking punch.

> **Remember that covering is a defensive manoeuvre that should be carried out for as short a time as possible. Once the immediate onslaught has passed, you should be ready to launch a counterattack.**

The defender is covering here, but his position is entirely negative – his eyes are not on his opponent, and his head is in a potentially illegal position.

COUNTERING

Countering is scoring when you have defended yourself successfully against an opponent's attack. Any defensive movement can be followed by a counter.

Types of counter

The punch you choose to counter with depends on which defence you used. Generally:

- defensive moves that leave both hands free are the easiest ones from which to counter
- after a block or parry, the hand not used in the defensive action will be the one to counter, or at least the one that begins the counterattack
- the punch a boxer faces most often is the left jab to the head – there are many ways to defend and counter this, several of which are illustrated here.

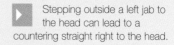
Stepping outside a left jab to the head can lead to a countering straight right to the head.

Coaching hints

- Aim to control punch speed and power in early practices, to make sure the counters are thrown correctly. As soon as you have grasped the correct 'feel' of the counter, you can increase the speed.
- Try straight punching first, then hooks, and lastly uppercuts.
- More advanced counters can be thrown either as single shots or combinations. The target can be switched from head to body, or body to head.
- Different types of opponent call for different counters, so practise against a variety of sparring partners.
- More aggressive styles should be able to defend and counter while moving forward.

Slipping inside a left jab followed by a right cross counter over the opponent's lead.

A countering left hook to the body can follow a slip inside a left jab to the head.

> **Skilful countering requires quick thinking, razor-sharp reactions and plenty of imagination – you need to be able to out-wit your opponent and respond to every opportunity.**

After pushing away from a left jab, push forward again and counter with your own left jab to the head.

Repeated counter punches to the body are a good way of wearing down an opponent.

INFIGHTING

The shorter the boxer, the more he will need to learn the art and craft of infighting – close-quarter boxing. Not only must he be able to move into the inside position and throw a variety of short-range punches, he must also learn how to move away in safety. His taller opponent will need to practise infighting too. His aim is to stop his opponent from scoring, and to move out of the close-quarter exchange as quickly as possible.

An upward surge lends force to a mid-range right uppercut.

You should practise a variety of punches individually and then in combinations – clusters of punches.

> The shorter aggressive-style boxer needs to gain the inside position and STAY THERE. Sustained pressure is the key.

Hooks and uppercuts should be thrown to both head and body. Being close to your opponent means that you cannot fully extend your arms – so greater emphasis is placed on twisting the trunk to increase power.

Getting inside

The boxer who gets his arms inside his opponent's generally controls the scoring at close quarters. From this position he can score while effectively preventing the opponent from scoring. However, care must be taken with this and the position of the head to ensure that the rules are not being infringed.

- Practise combinations from long to mid to short range, making sure that the front foot is in distance at each stage.
- Gaining the inside position – using either coach pads or partner work, practise defensive movements from the waist. Build from single counters to counter combinations.
- Conditioned spar – this could involve one partner acting as the 'backfoot defensive boxer' with the other trying to 'cut the ring off' and gaining the inside position.
- Pressure tactics – progress to applying sustained pressure by stringing two, three or more attacks together.
- Moving away safely – keep the guard high, vary the angles and go from short-range to long-range punches.

> The taller boxer's job is to keep it at long range, but he still needs to be able to 'look after himself' inside when he is closed down.

Uppercuts are some of the most effective moves in infighting. Try throwing them to both the head and the body.

COMBINATIONS

Having mastered the basic punches individually, combining them in clusters is the next step. A combination may contain two, three, four or more punches, and switch of attack. Timing, rhythm, speed and accuracy are essential.

'One-two'

The best known combination is the 'one-two' to the head, as shown below.

A southpaw boxer would throw the right hand first with the left following. The same combination can be delivered to the body.

Getting it right

To throw a successful combination:

- be careful to slide your feet into the correct position for the punch to follow – the feet must be in place before each part of the combination lands, if the timing is to be accurate

'One'– a light, measuring left jab is thrown at the target. It may make contact, or it may be just a feint.

'Two' – a fast straight right follows the jab, driven off the back foot with the right side pivoting through.

- keep your non-punching hand held on-guard
- stay relaxed to achieve speed and rhythm – power should be emphasised only in the final punch of a combination.

Coaching hints

- Shadowboxing (see page 49) is a good way of working out combinations – before sparring, it may help you decide which combination to try; after sparring, it can be used to go over and improve the combinations used.
- Practise the basic combinations taught by your coach, but also experiment

with developing your own – a wide range of combinations is a useful tool.

CLOSED TARGET

Beginning a combination with a jab has advantages, as has finishing the combination with the leading hand. Hence, the orthodox boxer might finish with a left hook and the southpaw with a right hook. This would 'close' the target, rather than leave it square-on and open to an opponent's attack.

A jab to the body, followed by a jab to the head, requires quick recovery between punches.

These photos show Amir Khan practising an advanced four-punch combination:

1 left jab to the head

2 counter-left hook to the body after slipping inside the opponent's jab

3 left hook to the head

4 right uppercut to the head.

SOUTHPAWS

Southpaw boxers follow all of the same technique points as orthodox boxers, though they will usually need to substitute 'left' for 'right', and vice-versa. Being in a minority to orthodox boxers, they are at an advantage when it comes to confusing an opponent.

FIGHT FEATURES

A contest between a southpaw and an orthodox boxer can look very different from a fight between two orthodox boxers. To the orthodox boxer a southpaw seems to be the 'wrong way round'.

Southpaw tricks

This southpaw has moved to the right to throw a 'long-range' right hook from outside his opponent's line of attack.

Leading with an aggressive right jab to the head.

Generally, southpaws are more used to fighting orthodox boxers than orthodox boxers are to fighting them. Southpaws should take advantage of this superior experience. In particular:

- southpaws need to develop the art of feinting an attack – the orthodox boxer will be confused as to which side a punch is coming from
- switching attack and changing direction will successfully add to the confusion
- sideways movements are very effective once an orthodox opponent's lead has been triggered off.

ORTHODOX TACTICS VS SOUTHPAWS

- Move left outside the line of attack.
- Counter the right jab with left hooks.
- Straight rights to the head and body are good stock tactics.
- If you are up against a typical counterpuncher make him lead by feinting – focus on countering the counter.
- Be aware that southpaw styles vary as much as orthodox and some southpaws are right handed, so moving left could mean moving into a strong right hook.

The southpaw straight left is an equivalent to the straight right of an orthodox boxer.

Coaching hints

- When feinting, watch your opponent's reaction to a punch. Then decide on your counter, knowing how he or she will react to the feint.

- Most orthodox boxers throw straight rights or left hooks against southpaws – be ready for either and practise your defences.

- Try to make your opponent move the way that suits you in the ring; control and dictate the bout with your footwork. Make your opponent move onto your favourite punch!

TRAINING

Not only must boxers be skilful, they also need to be fit. It's no good packing perfect punches if you don't have the strength and resilience to complete a bout. Training regimes for boxers should improve cardiovascular fitness and muscle power as well as technique.

 Practising the jab.

PEAK CONDITION

A boxer must have:

- stamina – to keep going in a contest without tiring
- speed – in punches, footwork and defensive moves
- strength – to power the explosive drive from the feet through the body to the fist itself
- coordination – to maintain balance and control movements
- a keen eye and mental agility – to spot openings and act quickly on them.

FITNESS PROGRAMME

There are five disciplines that will help a boxer achieve full fitness.

- Running (see page 48) – ranging from jogging, fartlek and sustained runs, to high-quality interval training and speed endurance runs.
- Circuit training (see page 48) – starting with individual and fixed-load circuits through to boxing-specific target circuits. Keep a training log to record progress.
- Gym work (see page 49) – from aerobic to anaerobic workouts. The build-up should be gradual, and skill should always take priority.
- Weight training – for the serious senior, a progressive strength programme is essential.
- Flexibility work.

SKILL ACQUISITION

Skills training will vary with a boxer's experience. Boxing is an open skill, so teaching sound technique is only part of the coach's work. He or she then has to ensure the techniques are practised in many situations and against many possible styles of opponent.

Skills are developed in a number of different ways:

- technical sparring (practising one technique)
- conditioned sparring (responding to varied situations)
- open sparring (developing thinking and tactical awareness)
- themed equipment work (tuned to the individual's strengths/weaknesses)
- pad work (skill practice with a coach/partner)
- drills (disciplined routines: individual and with a partner)
- video analysis (both watching and 'modelling' on top performers, and learning from personal mistakes).

Quality over quantity

Skills should be practised and repeated until they can be used smoothly and efficiently. Rounds should be timed, with set periods of recovery. However, when working on skills, a beginner should rest regularly – tiredness can lead to bad habits. It is best to practise only in good form – never sacrifice quality for quantity.

▼ The floor-to-ceiling ball is used to develop speed, accuracy and timing.

USING EQUIPMENT

Correct use of training equipment will help a boxer improve skills and fitness. Each piece of equipment offers a different challenge.

Maize ball

This is a balloon-shaped, head-sized punch bag, suspended from the ceiling by a chain. To use it:

- work mainly with straight punches; occasionally try hooks and uppercuts with either hand
- practise defensive moves as the ball swings: move in all directions, especially circling left and right, always remaining able to punch with either hand
- try two- and three-punch combinations, making sure your feet are in range before each punch.

Bagwork

When working with a traditional straight-sided punch bag:

- throw straight punches to the head and body, in line with the shoulders, striking the bag as it swings towards you
- try both single and combination punches, emphasising speed and power of attack
- vary the attack constantly, with an eye to doing the unexpected on occasion
- quality of punching is vital; feel the knuckle part of the closed glove landing solidly

- take care not to switch off when moving away from the bag.

Wall bag

Mounted on a wall, this punch bag does not swing. Use it for:

- judging distance
- changing angles of attack
- varying the angle and range of punches
- moving away (varied footwork patterns)
- close quarter/inside work.

Skipping

A skipping rope is excellent for improving fitness and coordination:

- try skipping to music – balance and footwork rhythm will be greatly aided
- keep your body as relaxed as possible; never watch your feet
- try alternate-leg and 'feet together' actions, with single and double turns of the rope
- vary your pattern of leg movements; skip in all directions.

SPARRING

Sparring is the most important part of a boxer's training programme – it puts all acquired skills to the test. Good boxers make sparring a regular part of their routine.

Sparring strategy

- Keep your sparring partner guessing; be selective when punching – reduce the power.
- Concentrate on doing the basics well; master straight punching first.
- Vary your moves, but keep the essentials – good balance and sound footwork.
- Try changing tactics in each round.
- Practise moves and tactics against a variety of sparring partners, as each opponent presents a different challenge.

COACHING
The advantage of having a coach is that he can spot your mistakes from outside the ring. He can then work with you on correcting these, and help you learn new moves. And, of course, he can praise you – it's good to be reminded of your strengths.

Sparring gives boxers practice in a ring. Head-guards are often worn for protection, to aid confidence and also to prepare amateur boxers for competition-wear. Heavy gloves may also be used to reduce risk of injury, and a gumshield is essential at all times.

COMPETITION

The ultimate test for many boxers is to box against an opponent in a competitive bout – to pit their wits and skills over three or four rounds against an opponent matched according to age, weight and experience. Competitive boxing is a challenging sport.

◀ Amateur tournaments give budding boxers the opportunity to compete from a young age.

AMATEUR TOURNAMENTS

Belonging to an official ABAE club enables competitors to box in inter-club tournaments. The ABAE organises national championships for seniors and juniors; it also organises novice championships. For schoolchildren, championships are run by the Schools Amateur Boxing Association (SABA). There are also the NACYP – National Association of Clubs for Young People – national championships for junior boxers.

Controlled competition

Safety is paramount in amateur boxing. The referee controls the bout and ensures that the rules are observed. Scoring is done by three to five judges, depending on whether the contest is on a 'club show' or a championship stage (for scoring, see page 11). Each boxer is allowed two seconds, one of whom advises him between rounds.

Competition hints

Only thorough and varied training can prepare you for the range of styles you might face. Thinking on your feet and quickly assessing an opponent's technique is also essential if you are to box in a confident way. Responses depend very much on the individual boxer, but here are a few different tactics you can try.

Against a tall opponent

- Always keep your target moving, using your feet and movement from your waist.
- Try to draw your opponent's lead by feinting, then step inside and counter to the body and head.
- Use the ring to cut your opponent off in the corners – move sideways as well as in a straight line.

Against a shorter opponent

- Concentrate on staying in the middle of the ring, away from the ropes. Work at the angles.
- Keep your opponent at long range with good use of the jab.
- Straight punching will allow you to use your height and reach.
- Launch an occasional surprise attack – but don't stay there.

Against a southpaw opponent

- Try to force the southpaw to lead, but keep moving.
- Circle away from a southpaw's stronger hand – usually the left one.
- Look for opportunities to throw a right-hand counter to the body or head.
- Try a left hook over a southpaw jab.

> **On the day of the contest THINK POSITIVE. Focus on what you are good at.**

Against a counterpuncher

- Try to make your opponent lead, by feinting or drawing.
- Focus on throwing the last punch in an exchange – counter a counter.
- Break your opponent's rhythm by changing tempo – don't let a counterpuncher settle.
- Try some sustained pressure with successions of quick-fire attacks.

▽ Boxers must be prepared to face opponents of varied size, speed and build.

FURTHER INFORMATION

USEFUL ADDRESSES

The Amateur Boxing Association of England Ltd (ABAE)

Paul King, CEO
Terry Edwards,
Performance Director
Colin Brown, Hon Secretary
Jubilee Stand
Crystal Palace National
Sports Centre
London SE19 2BB
Tel: 020 8778 0251
Fax: 020 8778 9324
email: hq@abae.co.uk

Irish ABA

Sean Crowley, Hon. Secretary
National Boxing Stadium
South Circular Road
Dublin 2
Ireland
Tel: 00 3531 4533371
Fax: 00 3531 4540777
email:
iaba@eircom.net

Welsh ABA

David Francis, Hon Secretary
Marcross Court
2 Old School Court
Marcross, Llantwit Major
Vale of Glamorgan CF61 1ZD
Wales
Tel: 01446 771 112
email: francisgas@dialstart.net

Amateur Boxing Scotland

Donald Campbell, Administrator
Strathdonan
High Street
Elgin IV30 1AH
Scotland
Tel: 01343 544718
email:
donald@absboxing.fsnet.co.uk

Schools ABA

Dudley Savill
11 Beaconsfield Road
Ealing
London W5 5JE
Tel: 020 8840 5519

Referees and Judges (England)

Ray Black
1129 Hessle High Road
Hull
Yorkshire HU4 6SB
Tel: 01482 354 098

Boxing Board of Control Ltd (Professional Boxing)

Simon Block,
General Secretary
The Old Library
Trinity Street
Cardiff CF10 1BH
Wales
Tel: 02920 367000
Fax: 02920 367019
email: sblock@bbbofc.com
website: www.bbbofc.com

GLOSSARY

ABAE Amateur Boxing Association of England. Established as the Amateur Boxing Association (ABA) in 1880, it is the oldest amateur boxing governing body in the world.

Amateur A person who has never competed for prize money, staked, bet or declared wager except for approved Trust Fund or sponsorship.

Belt A line drawn from the top of the hips across the navel, below which any punch is a foul.

Block The use of hands, elbows, forearms or shoulders to stop the punch from scoring.

Bout An amateur or professional boxing contest.

Caution To administer a caution to a boxer against fouls to ensure fair play and compliance with the rules.

Circuit training Series of general or specific exercises combined in a sequence to improve fitness. This could include fixed load, target, agility or power training.

Clerk of the scales A qualified referee or judge who assists the official in charge (OIC) at the weighing in of boxers prior to the bout.

Coach pads Hand-held target pads used to develop technical and tactical skills. Types of basic pads include hook and jab and coachspar.

Combination A sequence of two or more punches.

Corners A ring has four corners. Competitors will be in the red and blue corners and the other two are called neutral corners.

Countering A punch or series of punches thrown after a defence and in response to an attacking punch.

Counterpuncher A boxing style that favours waiting for an opponent to commit to an attack before countering. Many southpaws are counterpunchers.

Covering A defensive posture adopted by a boxer to allow him or her time to regain composure under a heavy attack.

Disqualification A boxer will be disqualified if he or she is given three warnings by the referee during a bout, or immediately for committing a serious infringement.

Dominant hand A boxer's strongest hand.

Fartlek training Literally means 'speed play'. It is a training method for running using various speeds and tempos.

Flash boxer An unorthodox and unpredictable style.

Flexibility Range of movement of joints and muscles.

Footwork Movement of boxer's feet for attacking and defensive manoeuvres and also for leverage for punching.

Foul There are a number of specific fouls – including headbutting, holding and the low blow. Committing any of these can result in a caution, warning or disqualification.

Guard Position of the hands, arms and chin. The optimum position for defence, attack and counter.

Gumshield Protective mouthpiece. This must be worn and if it is deliberately ejected one or two times, the boxer shall be cautioned and the third offence will warrant a warning.

Head-guard Protective headwear. Used in sparring and in competition by amateurs.

High-tempo A bustling style, relying on a high-volume punch rate to unsettle opponents.

Hook A bent-arm punch usually used as a counter punch.

Interval training High intensity work in the gym or running. For example, 8 x 200 metres sprints with 300 metres recovery jog between each sprint. It is during the recovery (the interval) that the training benefit takes place.

Judge There are three or five judges for each bout, seated at different sides of the ring. Their job is to score blows struck by the boxers.

Knockdown When any part of the body (other than the feet) is touching the floor or hanging helplessly on the ropes or part way through the ropes or, if in the opinion of the referee the boxer is not in a fit condition to continue boxing, he or she will receive a mandatory count of eight.

Knockout (KO) When a boxer has been knocked down and the referee has counted to ten and out.

Lead An attacking punch.

Lead hand The nearest hand to the opponent. If it is the left hand then the boxer is orthodox; if it is the right hand then the boxer is southpaw.

Medical card Every boxer holds a medical card which will show that he or she is medically fit to box and the results of all bouts during his or her career.

Mitts Usually leather, the protective gloves are thinner than boxing gloves and are used for equipment work, such as the bag.

Novice Beginner or boxer with limited experience.

Orthodox boxer Usually right-handed, this is a boxer who leads with his or her left hand with left foot and side facing the opponent.

Parrying A hand defence used to deflect attacking head or body punches.

PNF Proprioceptive neuromuscular facilitation – a form of stretching that involves a partner actively stretching the participant. It is particularly good for improving flexibility.

Punch bag The traditional training bag. It is often made of leather, with a foam filling and suspended from the ceiling by chains.

Push-away Defensive footwork action.

Reach The length of a boxer's outstretched arm.

Recorder Ensures that all medical cards are completed and results of bouts listed.

Recreational boxing Keep-fit boxing using all aspects of boxing training except sparring.

Referee The referee officiates in the ring, controlling the bout and ensuring that the boxers obey the rules and act in a sportsmanlike manner, dispensing cautions and warnings where necessary.

Ring The minimum size for the ring is 14 ft sq and the maximum size is 20 ft sq, measured inside the line of the ropes. In championships, the minimum size is 16 ft sq.

Round The duration of the bout intervals: 90 seconds for children; 2 minutes for amateur; 2–3 minutes for professional contests. There is a 1-minute rest between rounds.

Seconds The coach in the corner responsible for the boxer's safety. During the bout, the second administers help with recovery and offers tactical advice.

Shadowboxing Usually a solo activity, the boxer throws punches at an imaginary target or to a mirror.

Slipping Twisting movement at the waist which takes the head outside or inside an attacking punch.

Southpaw boxer Usually left-handed, this is a boxer who leads with his or her right hand with the right foot and side facing opponent.

Sparring Partner-work practice developing technical skills and tactical awareness. There are three types of sparring: technique, conditioned and open.

Stylist A boxer with a predominantly long-range defensive style. Also refers to a technically skilled boxer.

Switch attacks A combination of punches involving switching the attack from head to body or vice versa.

Target area The area of the body and head where, if delivered correctly, punches will score.

Telegraphing Preparatory movements that signal to an opponent that a punch or attack is about to be delivered.

Warning The referee will issue a warning to a boxer (and indicate this to the judges) for a severe foul or persistent fouling. This will result in a 1 point deduction in professional fights and 2 points awarded to the opponent for amateur bouts.

AMATEUR AND PROFESSIONAL WEIGHT CATEGORIES

AMATEUR (upper limits)

Light flyweight	106 lb (48kg)
Flyweight	112 lb (51kg)
Bantamweight	119 lb (54kg)
Featherweight	125 lb (57kg)
Lightweight	132 lb (60kg)
Light welterweight	141 lb (64kg)
Welterweight	152 lb (69kg)
Middleweight	165 lb (75kg)
Light heavyweight	178 lb (81kg)
Heavyweight	201 lb (91kg)
Super heavyweight	Over 201 lb (91kg)

PROFESSIONAL (upper limits)

Strawweight	105 lb (47.7kg)
Junior flyweight	108 lb (49kg)
Flyweight	112 lb (51kg)
Bantamweight	118 lb (53.5kg)
Super bantam weight	122 lb (55.3kg)
Featherweight	126 lb (57.1kg)
Super featherweight	130 lb (59kg)
Lightweight	135 lb (61.2kg)
Light welterweight	140 lb (63.5kg)
Welterweight	147 lb (66.7kg)
Junior middleweight	154 lb (70kg)
Middleweight	160 lb (72.6kg)
Super middleweight	168 lb (76.4kg)
Light heavyweight	175 lb (79.4kg)
Cruiserweight	200 lb (90.9kg)
Heavyweight	Over 200 lb (90.9kg)

GREAT BOXERS

There have been many charismatic and technically superb athletes in the sport of boxing. However, only a handful have done something unique in their sport and have earned the right to be called truly 'great'. Here are some of the greatest boxers to take to the ring, both international and home-grown British talent.

Muhammad Ali

Born: 17 January 1942,
Louisville, USA
Few can argue that Ali was the 'greatest of all time', even though he said this himself. Ali is the only heavyweight to have lifted the world title three times – in 1964 against Sonny Liston, in 1974 against George Foreman, and in 1978 against Leon Spinks. He is also one of the few athletes to have transcended their sport, undertaking an immense amount or work for the civil liberties movement among other causes. At one point he was indeed 'the most famous person on the face of the earth' (another modest quote from the man himself).

Henry Armstrong

Born: 12 December 1912,
Columbus, USA
(died 24 October 1988)
'Homicide Hank' is the only boxer ever to hold three world titles simultaneously (feather, light and welterweight division) – in an era when there was only one world title for each weight. He won 151 of his 181 professional bouts (101 of these by knockout).

Joe Louis

Born: 13 May 1914,
Lafayette, USA
(died 12 April 1981)
The 'Black Bomber' held the world heavyweight record for nearly 12 years (1937-1948), and made a division record 25 successful title defences during this time (he also served in the US Army during World War II). During his career he had 71 bouts, winning 68 (54 KOs) and losing 3.

Archie Moore

Born: 13 December 1913, Benoit, USA (died 9 December 1998)
The 'Old Mongoose' has knocked out more opponents than anyone else in the history of professional boxing – in his 229 bouts he won 194, a stunning 141 by knockout. He became light heavyweight champion in 1952 and held the title for nearly a decade. During his career he fought nine world champions including Ali and Rocky Marciano (he was the only boxer to do this).

Willie Pep

Born: 19 December 1922,
Hartford, USA
Willie 'Will 'o the wisp' Pep was renowned for his elusiveness in the ring; that and his unbeaten record of

230 professional wins (from 242 bouts). He won the featherweight title in 1952 and retained it for six years. Legend has it that he once won a round without throwing a punch.

Sugar Ray Robinson

Born: 3 May 1921, Ailey, USA
(died 12 April 1989)
'Sugar' Ray Robinson – born Walker Smith Jnr – is held by many in boxing as the greatest pound for pound boxer of all time. He holds many records in the sport, including being the first boxer to win a divisional world championship fives times (middleweight) and holding the world welterweight title from 1946 to 1951. His career record also makes impressive reading: 173 wins (109 KOs), 19 losses and 6 draws. Incredibly, Sugar Ray was never physically knocked out (although he did receive one technical KO).

Mickey Walker

Born: 13 July 1901, Elizabeth, USA
(died 28 April 1981)
Mickey 'The Toy Bulldog' Walker holds the honour as the boxer with the longest reign at two weights. In 1922, when he was just 21, he became world welterweight champion and held this until 1926 when he became world middleweight champion, a title he held until 1931. That's ten years at the top!

Sugar Ray Leonard

Born: 17 May 1956, Wilmington, USA
'Sugar' Ray Leonard was Boxer of the Decade for the 1980s – he entered the decade a champion and left it a champion. During this time he also became the first boxer to win five world titles in five weight classes. Leonard was a skilled boxer in the ring, but his strength lay in his ability to analyse opponents before a bout and devise strategies to overcome them.

Thomas Hearns

Born: 18 October 1958, Memphis, USA
Thomas 'The Hitman' Hearns stakes his claim as one of the greatest by being the first boxer to win seven world titles (six of which were at different weight divisions). He also has an impressive career record of 59 wins (48 KOs) from 64 fights with just 4 defeats (two of which were great bouts against Sugar Ray Leonard and Marvin Hagler).

GREAT BRITONS

Bob Fitzsimmons

Born: 26 May 1863, Helston, England
(died 22 October 1917)
'Ruby Robert' was the first boxer to hold world titles at three weights: middle, heavy and light heavy (in that order). His long career often saw him in bouts against boxers much heavier than himself, and he had to rely on the power of his punches – which had a fearsome reputation.

Jimmy Wilde

Born: 15 May 1892, Merthyr Tydfil, Wales (died 10 March 1969)
Jimmy Wilde's list of nicknames is almost as impressive as his record –

'The Mighty Atom', 'The Tylorstown Terror' and 'The Ghost with a Hammer in His Hand'. Jimmy never weighed in at more than 108 lb (49kg) for any of his professional fights. Despite this, he was exceptionally strong and fast – attributes that helped him on his way to a career record of 149 fights with only 4 losses (he had a winning run of 101 bouts!). At his peak he was World Flyweight Champion.

ONES TO WATCH...

Ricky Hatton

Born: 6 October 1978, Stockport, England.
Known as 'The Hitman', Ricky Hatton is the reigning and undefeated IBF light-welterweight world champion. He recently added the WBA belt to his collection, taking his record to an impressive 40 wins (30 by knockout) and no losses. Ricky is known for his quiet and modest manner outside the ring, but once he steps through the ropes he has a devastating all-action style and powerful left hook.

Amir Khan

Born: 8 December 1986, Bolton, England.
Amir is one of the most talented amateurs to emerge from Britain in many years. He burst onto the public scene by winning Silver at the 2004 Olympic Games in Athens, losing out to the superb amateur champion Mario Kinderlan of Cuba. Khan beat Kinderlan in a rematch, which was his last fight as an amateur. He has now embarked on a professional career and the early signs are promising.

INDEX